PAID FOR WITH
GAT FUNDS

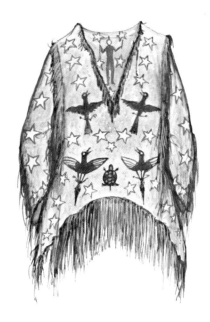

The Civilization Library
Published in the United States by
Gloucester Press in 1978

Originated and designed by
David Cook and Associates
and produced by
The Archon Press Ltd
28 Percy Street
London W1P 9FF

First published in
Great Britain 1977 by
Hamish Hamilton
Children's Books Ltd
90 Great Russell Street
London WC1B 3PT

Printed in Italy
by Alfieri & Lacroix

Library of Congress Cataloging in Publication Data

Davis, Christopher, 1928-
  Plains Indians.

  (The Civilization library)
  Includes index.
  SUMMARY: Discusses the Great Plains of the
United States and the Indians who inhabited the
land.
  1. Indians of North America—Great Plains—Juve-
nile literature. [1. Indians of North America—Great
Plains. 2. Great Plains] I. Wilson, Maurice Charles
John, 1914- II. Thompson, George William, 1925-
III. Title. IV. Series.
E78.G73D38   978'.004'97   77-12087
ISBN 0-531-01429-0

THE CIVILIZATION LIBRARY

PLAINS INDIANS

Christopher Davis

Special Consultant
J. C. H. King,
of the Museum of Mankind, London

Illustrated by

Maurice Wilson and George Thompson

Gloucester Press · New York · 1978

Peoples of the Great Plains

The Great Plains of North America stretch on endlessly—a flat, empty sea of grass. In summer, they bake under a fiery sun; there are sudden storms and tornadoes. In winter, freezing winds drive snow across them, piling it in ghostly drifts. The sky is all around—big and close as if pressing down on the earth.

These vast grasslands were once the home and hunting ground of the tribes of native North Americans called the Plains Indians. Indians had lived on the Plains since prehistoric times, but the high point of their society, and the period of this book, lasted only 200 years. In that time, beneath the Big Sky (as they called it), they lived a life that is no longer possible. They rode, hunted, danced, dreamed, warred and lived in harmony with the land and the natural world around them. This life depended on two animals—the horse and the buffalo.

The Great Plains
There are almost a million square miles of the Plains, including all or parts of 13 states, and 3 Canadian provinces.

Faces of the Plains
Each tribe had a different style of hair and headdress. The feathered warbonnet worn in some tribes stood for great achievements. Some chiefs wore just a single feather—as Sitting Bull does here.

Sioux

Pawnee

Kansa

Blackfoot

4

It began in the late 17th century when the Indians obtained large herds of horses from the Spaniards. (The Spanish were the first Europeans to explore this part of America, and they brought the horse with them.) It ended in the late 19th century, with the killing of the last of the buffalo, on which the tribes depended.

In those 200 years, two separate groups of tribes lived on the Plains. The first were the village tribes who farmed, and lived most of the year in villages: the Mandan, Hidatsa, Arikara, Pawnee, Osage, Oto, Omaha, Ponca, Wichita, Missouri, Kansa, Iowa. The others were the wandering, or nomadic tribes, who roamed the Plains, living in tepees and who held out the longest against the white invasion of the West: the Cheyenne, Arapaho, Crow, Comanche, Blackfoot, Kiowa, Assiniboin, Cree, Gros Ventre and the many divisions of the Sioux nation.

Tribal Lands

The Great Plains stretch from the Mississippi River to the foothills of the Rocky Mountains, from the Saskatchewan River Basin in Canada, down almost to the Rio Grande in Texas. They can be divided into two sections—the Prairies or Tall Grass Plains (light green), and the High Plains or Short Grass Plains (yellow). Both regions are mostly flat and treeless, except for the Black Hills of South Dakota, the Sandhills of Nebraska, and the Wichita Mountains of Oklahoma (dark green areas). The map shows where the major tribes lived at the height of their horse-riding, buffalo-hunting culture— 1680–1890. The village tribes settled on the eastern edges of the Plains. The nomadic tribes traveled the western and central regions.

Hunting the buffalo

Nobody knows how many buffalo once roamed the Plains—perhaps as many as 60 million. There are reports of huge herds blackening the Plains as far as the eye could see. In winter the buffalo migrated south a few hundred miles; in summer they returned, but never by the same trails. They were a mystery. The hunters couldn't lie in wait for them because no one knew when they would return, or by what path. But they always came. Scouts would spot them, and the first summer hunt would begin.

At the start of warm weather the tribes gathered together on the Plains and tribal discipline (which was loose in winter) became very strict. There were harsh punishments for those who broke rules. Many tribes named hunt leaders to enforce them. They were afraid that a young hunter too eager for glory might scare the herd and cause a stampede that would ruin the hunt.

Hunting on horseback

Buffalo hunting took strength, skill and daring. A full-grown bull could weigh 200 pounds and stand 6 feet high at the shoulder. The favorite way of hunting was the "surround." The hunters formed a circle around the herd, making it disorganized and fearful. Then they rode in for the kill, aiming their lances and arrows at a spot behind the buffalo's shoulder blades, and piercing the heart.

The hunters decorated their buffalo ponies with feathers and bead embroidery. Ponies were picked for speed and endurance. With a short start, a buffalo can outrun a horse. Even badly wounded, a buffalo may run a mile before it drops. The ponies were trained to veer away from the buffalo's horns, and not to panic if the herd stampeded.

It was hard to guess how buffalo would behave. Sometimes the herd would not seem to notice the hunters, even though a buffalo was killed. At other times, the whole herd would stampede for no reason. It was a dangerous sport for the hunters, but to win meant food, clothing, and survival.

Before the hunt the Indians praised the spirit of the buffalo. When the hunt was over, they cut out the livers of the dead buffalo and ate them raw. They also cut out the hearts and left them on the Plains—believing this would bring new life to the herd.

Hunting on foot
Originally the Indians hunted buffalo on foot. A hunter wearing a wolfskin could sneak up on the herd. Healthy buffalo did not fear wolves or any other animals, so this disguise was successful.

Sometimes the Indians built a fenced-in area. Then they set fire to the grass behind the buffalo, driving them toward the corral. Indians on either side of the herd screamed and waved robes, forcing the buffalo into the trap.

Another method was to force the herd to stampede over a cliff. Several hundred animals could be killed in this way. It was still used after the tribes had horses.

The life-giver

The Indian women cut up the buffalo, and they wasted nothing. Every part of the animal was used. Even the dung was dried for fuel. The liver, kidneys, brain and bone marrow were eaten raw; the flesh was boiled in water or roasted over a fire. Any extra meat was sliced into thin strips and then smoked or dried in the sun. This "jerky" would keep for a long time. Another way to store the meat was to make "pemmican." For this, dried meat was pounded with crushed berries. Then grease and marrow were poured over it to seal it. This was eaten all winter.

Buffalo hide had many uses. An old bull's thick hide was used for shields and moccasin soles, cowhide made tepee coverings, and both were used for clothing. Horns and hoofs were made into bowls, spoons and powder-horns. Intestines became buckets and cooking vessels. Shoulder blades made hoes, hair was woven into rope or stuffed into pillows, sinews made bowstrings or thread, fat made soap, and tails became fly swatters. Bones made knives, necklaces, dice and paintbrushes. Even the rough side of the tongue was used—as a hairbrush.

A hanging kettle
Some tribes used a buffalo paunch (stomach-lining) as a kettle or bucket for cooking meat. They put in the meat and water, then added hot stones.

Hides and meat
Buffalo skins were stretched out on the ground to bleach in the sun. The women scraped them to an even thickness. Autumn was the time for doing this, and for drying meat—"jerky"—on racks, for the winter.

8

Sioux woman

Mandan chief

Assiniboin girl

Hidatsa warrior

Clothes and calendars

Buffalo hide could be made into
almost any kind of clothing—
although deerskin was preferred.
Hide with hair made warm robes,
capes, caps and mittens. Hide without
hair made underclothes, shirts,
dresses, leggings and moccasins. A
warrior's robe like the Cheyenne robe,
right, was often decorated with
picture writing—"pictographs"—
that told of his deeds in battle or
showed a war scene. Some robes
became calendars, picturing important
events of the past. They were the
tribe's only historical records, except
for spoken stories.

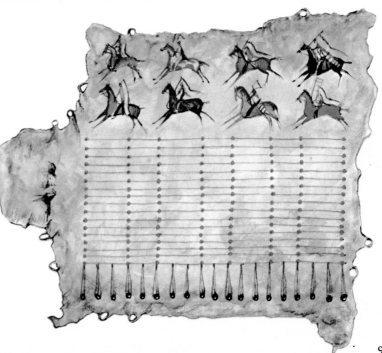

The wealth of horses

Bridles
The common or war bridle (top) was a rope tied around the horse's lower jaw. The bridle below was used for an unbroken horse.

Wild horses
Mustangs were horses that had bred wild on the Plains. The Indians often chased them in teams, hoping to wear them out and then lasso them.

In the 16th century, the Spaniards arrived in southwestern America, bringing the horse. The Indians were amazed; their only beast of burden was the dog. They called the horse Medicine Dog, Big Dog, or God Dog. It became a valued possession and completely changed their lives. Hunting became easier and more profitable; they could kill more buffalo than they needed. Their warring became more deadly. Some tribes, like the Cheyenne, gave up settled lives as farmers, and became warriors and hunters. Tribes now raided each other frequently—more often to steal horses than to fight. Great honor was given to a rider who could steal horses from under the noses of a rival tribe.

Tribes that had crossed the plains slowly on foot now traveled great distances, carrying lots of supplies. Their tepees were bigger, and were stocked with buffalo meat and

skins, and the goods they needed for barter. Horses became a sign of wealth. Those who owned many felt safe; they could hunt and defend themselves. Some chiefs had 200; and a young warrior needed to build a herd if he hoped to marry well, for horses were given to the bride's father to show respect for the bride.

The Plains Indians adapted to horses quickly. They trained them for buffalo hunts and for war, and learned to breed them. They learned to ride almost as soon as they could walk. Indian warriors have been called the best horse-soldiers in the world. The Sioux and Comanche were probably the most skilled and feared. Comanches were said to ride more naturally than they walked. When a warrior died, the heads and tails of his favorite horses were sometimes placed near him—to help him travel in the afterlife.

Trading

Horses spread through the Plains tribes in the 17th and 18th centuries. At first, the Spanish traded a few to the tribes. Then in 1680, the Pueblo Indians in New Mexico revolted against the Spanish and captured several thousand horses.

Southwestern tribes that had horses traded them to tribes in the northeast that had no horses, but had guns (acquired from the French and English in exchange for furs). In time, each tribe became mounted. A horse—the Indian's most prized possession—might be traded for a gun with ammunition, tobacco, a decorated shirt and leggings, 3 metal knives, a bear-claw necklace, 2 buffalo robes, 5 tepee poles, a tepee cover and some small skins and eagle feathers.

Years of plenty

All summer great herds of buffalo supplied meat for the tribes. The Great Plains provided many wild foods. Berries and fruits—grapes, chokecherries and plums—grew wild in the region. Some were dried and powdered or mixed with dried buffalo meat for use during the winter, when the buffalo moved south. Wild rice, onions, peas, acorns and prickly pears were plentiful. The pears were sometimes sliced and added to buffalo soups and stews. Herbs, such as sage, were also added. The wild turnip was a prized delicacy. It could be eaten fresh, baked in hot ashes, or it could be dried and preserved.

Both the nomadic tribes and the village tribes hunted buffalo, but the village tribes also farmed. In the spring they planted corn, beans, squash, pumpkins and sunflowers; then all but the old or sick left the village to join the yearly

Wild plants

Wild turnips, sage, cherries and rose hips grew on the Plains. The tribes gathered everything that could be eaten in case one day the buffalo did not return. They needed the variety—and the vitamins—fruits and berries gave them.

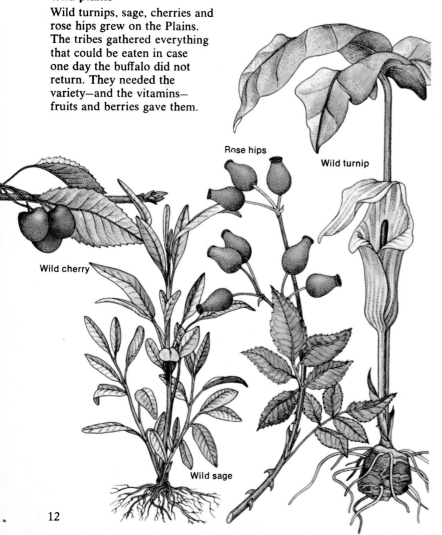

Rose hips

Wild turnip

Wild cherry

Wild sage

Animals of the Plains

In the early years of the Plains Indians, there were many antelope. In northern valleys lived elk, deer and bear. Buckskin was used for clothing and antlers for tools and knife handles.

Elk supplied meat, hides and antler-horn.

Jack rabbits were eaten. Their fur made trimmings.

Raccoon fur was also used for trimming.

buffalo hunt. At harvest time, in late summer, they returned. If the harvest was good, they traded extra vegetables to the nomadic tribes for meat and hides. What the village tribes did not eat or trade, they stored in jug-shaped pits up to eight feet deep. The pits were entered by ladder, and the entrances were concealed by ashes and grass.

To some nomadic tribes fish were taboo (forbidden), and others fished only when food was scarce. But the village tribes who lived near rivers caught fish in many different ways. The Cree built fences in the river, then scooped up the fish and clubbed them. The Blackfoot made wooden basket cages; the Omaha used arrows or harpoons. In winter the village tribes hunted on the frozen lakes. Wearing snowshoes, they chased antelope and other animals, and killed them as they skidded on the ice.

Chief of birds
The Golden Eagle's feathers were used in warriors' headdresses. A hunter hid in a pit, using meat for bait. When the bird swooped down, he killed it with his hands.

Gathering and growing
Usually Indian women gathered the wild roots and berries; grew crops; cooked, preserved and stored food. They used hoes made from buffalo shoulder blades, and rakes made from horn.

Tepees

The nomadic tribes set up their tepees in a circle or semi-circle. The women put them up and were usually considered their owners. To make a tepee, buffalo hides were sewn together with sinew and wrapped around a frame of poles. Two poles were attached to flaps at the top which could be closed. So could the entrance, which had a skin curtain. The fireplace was in the center of the tepee, with a smoke vent above it. The place of honor was at the rear, facing the entrance.

14

Tepees and lodges

All the Plains Indians used the tepee—the nomadic tribes lived in them all the time; the village tribes used them on hunting trips. Tepees were roomy, comfortable, easy to set up, cool in summer, warm in winter, waterproof and portable. When the outside was painted with magic symbols or the deeds of its warrior-owner they were beautiful as well. Size varied by region: the Crows could find tall pine trees and used supporting poles of up to 30 feet that stretched high above the hide covering. An average tepee in the northern Plains was about 10 feet high, with a base 15 feet around. This tepee would need 15 to 20 hides to cover it. In the southern Plains, wood was scarcer and tepees smaller.

When they were not hunting, the village tribes lived in semi-permanent homes. The Pawnee, Omaha, Arikara, Mandan, and Hidatsa built sturdy, round, earth lodges; the Wichita made grass lodges. The Osage built oval, domed houses covered with skins or mats. These dwellings were usually near water, and the settlements were often protected by a ditch and a high fence.

Earth lodges

A lodge could hold a "family" of 40 people. It had a covered entrance leading to one big room. Smoke from the fireplace escaped through a hole in the roof. Earth benches or platforms of sticks served as beds. The walls and roof were covered with branches, grass, sod and earth.

The nomad's life

The nomadic tribes moved constantly—seeking sheltered places in winter, good water supplies in summer; following the buffalo herds; fleeing from enemy attacks. Before they had horses, they might travel six miles a day, taking with them only what the women and dogs could carry. The men carried only weapons, to be ready in case of attack. With horses, the tribes could cover thirty miles a day and carry all their possessions with them. The horse, like the dog, was used as a pack animal.

Belongings were carried on "travois" that were made and owned by the women of the tribe. A travois was made by fastening two poles together at the animal's shoulders, with the other ends dragging behind. A frame or net was

stretched between the poles to carry a load of meat, clothes and utensils. Other belongings were packed into saddlebags, or large rawhide envelopes called "parfleches" that were strapped to the sides of a horse. Travois were also used to carry those who were old or sick. Before the horse they might have been left behind. Small children sometimes rode in a wooden pen on a travois.

Tribes using horses could travel hundreds of miles to barter for new, interesting goods. Enemy tribes even declared truces in order to trade peacefully. Tribes who spoke different languages communicated by using sign language. Hand signals were understood by all, as were the smoke signals war parties used to send messages.

Moving camp
"Travois," pulled by dogs and horses, carry the possessions of a group of Blackfoot. A horse travois holds a wooden pen for two children. In the background are burial platforms. In some areas, the dead were buried in the ground. In others, they were wrapped in blankets and placed on a platform with their treasured belongings.

Growing up

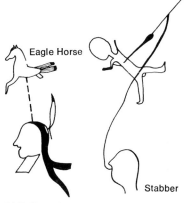

Eagle Horse

Stabber

Childhood
Names were sometimes written in pictographs (above). Children were included in the life of the tribe at an early age. A child was strapped onto a horse at age two or three.

The Plains Indians treated their children with affection, respect and understanding. They did not hit their children, and never understood why some white people did. But they did not spoil them, and encouraged them to be strong and self-disciplined from an early age so they could survive the hardships of nomadic life: the times when food was scarce, game hard to find, and the cold painful; and the times when the tribe was struck by war or disease. An Indian had to face these possibilities.

An Indian infant was not allowed to cry. If a child continued crying after it was fed and fondled, the mother hung it in its cradleboard (a wooden carrier) on a bush away from camp until it stopped. There was an important reason for this—a crying child could give away the tribe's hiding place to its enemies.

The most important goal in a Plains Indian's life was not to be tough and brave, but to win the approval of the rest of the tribe. Disapproval brought harsh punishment—especially if the tribe had been endangered.

Children were usually named by relatives or elders of the tribe. A boy's name often described a brave act or famous battle. Girls usually kept their names all their lives. A boy might change his if he performed a special act of bravery, or if a vision or dream led him to take a new name.

As the young Indians began to grow up, the boys and girls were kept more apart. The tribe began to prepare them for their adult roles. A boy would seek his guardian spirit and would go on his first hunt. Then he would go on a raid and gradually take on the warrior's way of life—learning the skills of war and horsemanship.

Sweat lodges

These were used as baths, or to purify the body and soul. They were also used for story-telling and teaching the young the ways of the tribe. A frame of willow, covered with buffalo hide, was set up over a fireplace. Red-hot rocks were put in the fireplace and water was poured over them, making the lodge a hot, dark steam-room.

A deadly game

When a boy approached manhood, he left his village for a time to search for his guardian spirit. He fasted, prayed, and sometimes even cut off a finger in order to reach a delirious state in which a vision came to him. The vision told him to collect special objects and roll them up to make his own medicine bundle. On his first war raid, he hoped to prove his bundle held "strong" medicine. A brave warrior was one of the tribe's most respected members; a warrior's death was the noblest way to die.

Warfare among the Plains tribes often seemed more like a game than a battle, but it could be deadly. The aim of many raids was not to kill, but to count "coup"—touch an enemy with a "coup stick." But in some tribes, counting coup also meant stealing a horse or a weapon or taking a scalp. Scalp raids were usually inspired by grief, or aimed at revenge. Unlike scalp raiders, horse raiders went on foot—hoping to ride home on captured horses.

After a successful raid, the warriors paraded through camp, showing their booty to the tribe. If a young warrior died, the tribe mourned, and the widow scratched herself with thorns, cut her hair, and sometimes cut off one of her fingers, as signs of grief.

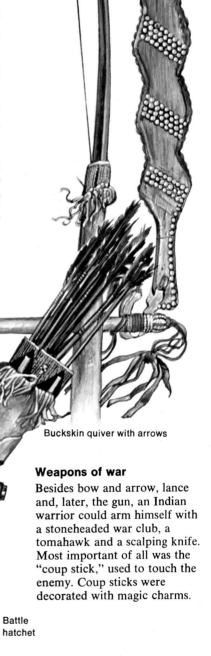

Warrior's bow   Coup stick

War club

Stuffed kingfisher

War knife

Buckskin quiver with arrows

Battle hatchet

Weapons of war
Besides bow and arrow, lance and, later, the gun, an Indian warrior could arm himself with a stoneheaded war club, a tomahawk and a scalping knife. Most important of all was the "coup stick," used to touch the enemy. Coup sticks were decorated with magic charms.

A warrior

The warrior, a Blackfoot, is dressed and armed for war. The paint on his face, his warbonnet, the designs on his clothes and on the harness are all part of his personal "medicine." He believes this will give him strength and protection, and frighten his enemies. Before a raid, warriors went through long ceremonies, hoping for a sign or vision that they would win.

21

Peacetime activities

Games and sports were popular among the Plains tribes. They raced each other on foot and on horseback, wrestled and competed at archery. Young children played at grown-up roles—boys rode stick horses, girls set up miniature tepees. As they grew older, the boys started using real horses. The Sioux played "throwing-them-off-their-horses," a rough game in which they tried to wrestle each other off their mounts. This toughened them as warriors, and helped develop their riding skills.

The adults often gambled. A reckless man might bet his horses or even his wives on the result of any contest, from a horse race to a game of dice played with plum pits. The most popular game among the women was probably "shinny," a kind of field hockey played with sticks and a ball of buckskin.

Sports and games

The hoop and pole game was a favorite of the men of the tribe. Two players rolled a hoop along the ground and then threw darts, arrows or long poles at it. The game of lacrosse was also popular with the Sioux, Cheyenne and Assiniboin. Sometimes several hundred players joined in.

MWilson

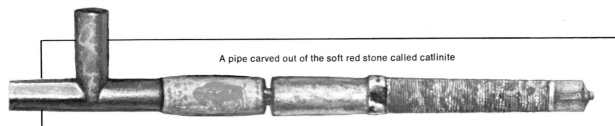

A pipe carved out of the soft red stone called catlinite

Pipes and smoking

Smoking was a serious activity among the Indians. No decision of peace or war, of business or tribal affairs, was made without a pipe-smoking ceremony. The Indians believed a pipe put them in touch with the spirit world, and that the smoke they blew out was a prayer.

Probably all the Plains tribes smoked; but not all grew tobacco. Pipes were carved in many forms and a good one was treasured.

Ceremonial pipe decorated with glass beads, wool and horsehair.

The Buffalo Dance

The Mandan tribe held a Buffalo Dance to attract the herds of buffalo. The dancers took the roles of hunters and animals, in imitation of the hunt.

Dreamers beneath the Big Sky

The Sun Dance was the most important ceremony of the Plains Indians. Dreams and visions had always been part of tribal life. The ceremony of the Sun Dance expressed their spiritual feelings about the mysteries of the Big Sky and the endless plains.

The Dance was usually held in midsummer, when the tribes gathered for the buffalo hunt. It was often called by young men who wanted to avenge a loved one's death, or to regain their honor after a shameful act. The young men— the dancers—fasted, while the tribe feasted on buffalo tongue. A buffalo hide was hung on the center pole of the Sun Dance Lodge. The pole was a tree that had been "killed" (cut) with great ceremony. The dancers pushed sharpened sticks through the skin of their backs or chests. Leather strips tied these sharp sticks—and the dancers—to the center pole.

Slowly, the dancers moved to a drum beat—pulling back from the pole, trying to tear themselves free. In order to prove their courage they danced without food or water, and endured great pain. The Sun Dance lasted from sunrise to sunset, or until the dancers fell into a trance or had a vision.

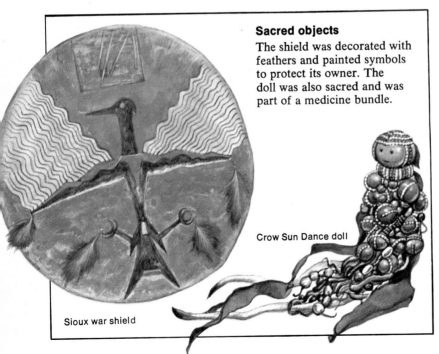

Sacred objects
The shield was decorated with feathers and painted symbols to protect its owner. The doll was also sacred and was part of a medicine bundle.

Crow Sun Dance doll

Sioux war shield

Arapaho Sun Dance

The Plains Wars

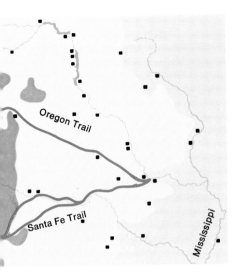

Once the white people started pushing west for land and gold, the Great Plains tribes were in danger. The pioneers killed or drove away the buffalo, and their trails crossed the Indian hunting grounds. They also brought disease: smallpox nearly wiped out the Mandan and Hidatsa; cholera swept through the Blackfoot, Cheyenne, Kiowa and Comanche.

And, the United States government was forcing the tribes to sell their land. The tribes united for protection. In 1851, at Horse Creek, Wyoming, 10,000 gathered and signed a treaty with the government. In return for giving travelers safe passage on the trails, Indian hunting grounds were to be preserved.

The drive west (above)

Trails and forts (the black squares) of the white people spread across the northern part of the Plains. At first only a few pioneers pushed their way along the trails, but every year there were more. When word spread of gold in the west, there was a great rush of people. All this time the buffalo were disappearing—thousands of them were killed by the white people.

A broken peace

In 1864 the army broke a pact and attacked the Cheyenne camp at Sand Creek. Many Indians— including women and children— were killed. The Cheyenne then joined the Sioux and Arapaho in attacking white stagecoach stations and ranches.

Peace lasted just three years. Then, after a white settler complained of a stolen cow, an army force attacked a Sioux camp and was wiped out. The Plains Wars, which were to last for 36 years, had begun. Their real cause was the white invasion of tribal lands.

There were many battles. The Cheyenne tried to stop the building of the "Iron Horse" (the railroad) through their hunting grounds. The Oglala Sioux refused to give safe passage through their land.

Finally, the government ordered the Sioux to move from the Black Hills, in spite of a treaty giving them the land for all time. It was one of hundreds of broken treaties, and led to the last war on the Plains.

Outbreak of war

In 1854, a Mormon settler reported a cow stolen by the Miniconjou Sioux, who said the cow was lame and had been abandoned. But the army attacked the Sioux camp and the Plains wars began.

Final defeat

The end of freedom

Soon after the battle of Little Big Horn, Crazy Horse and the Oglala Sioux surrendered. Sitting Bull also gave himself up. Both chiefs were later killed. The Northern Cheyenne were sent to a dismal reservation in Oklahoma. They refused to stay, but were recaptured by the army. The tribes longed for their lost freedom. Ten Bears, a Comanche chief, said, "I was born on the prairie where the wind blew free and there was nothing to break the light of the sun. I was born where there were no enclosures and where everything drew a deep breath. I want to die there and not within walls."

To the Sioux, the Black Hills (in what is now South Dakota) were sacred. They refused to move so prospectors could look for gold, and the army was sent to round them up.

On the march to the Black Hills, the army attacked a Cheyenne camp. Cheyenne warriors then joined two groups of Sioux led by Crazy Horse and Sitting Bull. Crazy Horse stopped the army's first major attack at Rosebud Creek, and then camped with many warriors on Little Big Horn River. General Custer and a small group of soldiers discovered the Indian camp and attacked. The soldiers were surrounded and quickly killed. It was the Indians' greatest victory—and their last.

From then on, the Plains Indians were forced onto reservations. There they had no buffalo to hunt or to eat, no war parties, and no excitement. They were often hungry and had to depend on the government for food. All they could do was dream of the past, or of a better future.

MWilson

It was a dream that set off the last act of defiance. In 1890 news spread through the tribes of an Indian named Wovoka who had had a vision during an eclipse of the sun. He said he had seen dead Indians rising from the land, and buffalo returning to the Plains. The Great Spirit had told him this dream would come true and the whites would leave the land if the people danced the Ghost Dance.

This message of hope raced through the tribes on the reservations. All across the Plains they danced the Ghost Dance. The white people were frightened by the dance fever. On December 29, 1890, a large band of Sioux, many wearing Ghost Shirts, which they believed would protect them from bullets, were met by the army. The army ordered them to hand over their weapons. The Sioux refused, and were shot down. Several hundred men, women and children were killed. The Ghost Shirts had not protected them, and the Indians' dream was over.

Arapaho woman's Ghost Shirt

The Ghost Dance

This Dance was the last attempt by the Plains Indians to restore their way of life. Most of the tribes had been on reservations for 10 years, and they were in despair. They believed that by dancing the Ghost Dance they could bring dead warriors back to life and make the buffalo herds return. They wore Ghost Shirts which they thought would protect them from the soldier's bullets. When Big Foot's band of Sioux, wearing Ghost Shirts, were killed at Wounded Knee in 1890, the Ghost religion ended.

Living in a changed world

On the Plains there is still the Big Sky, and huge stretches of grassland. There are also towns and roads and telephone wires—and no Indians. The empty spaces ring with ghostly echoes of hoofs and drum beats and whistling arrows. Most Indians are on reservations now, on land white people did not want. They do not hunt, for there is no game. They farm a little and some tribes have small industries. But most must depend on the government for help.

It is hard for them. They gave up a way of life that had little to do with money and property. It was centered about the Earth, which they believed to be their mother. Some still look back to the old days of the buffalo and horse. Others, knowing that this life will not come again, look ahead and try to make a new kind of life. But many still want to be Indian—to learn tribal dances and language and history, to live freely and proudly once more.

31

Index